THINGS TO TRANSLATE

PIOTR SOMMER

THINGS TO TRANSLATE
& OTHER POEMS

TRANSLATED BY
PIOTR SOMMER
&
ED ADAMS
JOHN ASHBERY
DOUGLAS DUNN
D.J. ENRIGHT
MICHAEL KASPER
CHARLES MIGNON
ELŻBIETA VOLKMER

BLOODAXE BOOKS

ISBN: 1 85224 155 1

First published 1991 by
Bloodaxe Books Ltd,
P.O. Box 1SN,
Newcastle upon Tyne NE99 1SN.

Acknowledgements are due to the Arts Council
for providing a translation grant for this book.

Bloodaxe Books Ltd acknowledges
the financial assistance of Northern Arts.

Cover reproduction by V & H Reprographics, Newcastle upon Tyne.

Printed in Great Britain by
Billing & Sons Limited, Worcester.

Acknowledgements

Acknowledgements are due to the editors of the following publications in which some of these translations (since modified) first appeared: *The Faber Book of Fevers and Frets* (Faber, 1989), *Fortnight, The Honest Ulsterman, International Portland Review, Ploughshares, The Poetry Miscellany, Stone Ferry Review, Storm,* and *The Times Literary Supplement.* The prose sequence *Things to Translate* (written in English) first appeared in *The Threepenny Review.*

The book includes poems which seemed translatable enough to be used at readings which I've sporadically given since the late seventies; translatable enough, that is, without losing all their Polish tonalities. Readings were in fact the only reason why some of the poems were dragged from the Polish into English in the first place.

Regular contact with my co-translators wasn't always feasible in those days. From the moment when – thanks to them – batches of unfinished half-literals started to turn into a more orderly manuscript, other friends, natives of both British and American English, have also seen them. Of those whose comments and suggestions at different stages helped me to improve the manuscript, I'm especially grateful to Roger Boyes, Marianne Craven, Tamara Duvall, Emma Harris, Deborah Eisenberg and Wallace Shawn, Michael Hofmann, August Kleinzahler, Joanna Labon, Kristin and Barry O'Connell, Caryl Phillips, Felicity Rosslyn, Mark Slobin, David Sofield, Susan Sontag and Mark Stevens. Without their help the experiment would have been substantially poorer.

Special thanks are also due to Krzysztof Franczak for his assistance with the photographs of Otwock.

P.S.

Contents

LYRIC FACTOR & OTHER POEMS
CZYNNIK LIRYCZNY I INNE WIERSZE
(1988)

Indiscretions

Where are we? In ironies
that no one will grasp, short-lived
and unmarked, in trivial points
which reduce metaphysics to absurd
detail, in Tuesday that falls on
day two of May, in mnemonics of days.
You can give an example or take it
on faith, cat's paw at the throat.

And one also likes certain words and those – pardon me –
syntaxes that pretend that something links them together.
Between these intermeanings the whole man is contained,
squeezing in where he sees a little space.

[PS/DJE]

Candle

Friends from long ago, loved unchangingly,
with whom you could talk, talk until exhausted –
well, they must have forgotten some mutual concern,
or potentially mutual.
And new ones? New ones keep quiet,
as if they wanted to say nothing
more than necessary.

[PS/DJE]

Amnesia

I forgot about the other world.
I wake up with my mouth closed,
I wash the fruit with my mouth closed,
with a smile, I bring the fruit into the room.
I don't know why I remember cod-liver oil,
whole years of misery, the cellar bolt on the floor,
the self-sufficient voice of the grandmother.
Still, this is not the other-world.
And again I sit at the table with my mouth closed
and you bring me delicious bursting plums
and I repeat after someone I also forget:
there is no other world.

[EV/PS]

Stitch

Station lights connect with those above,
the days of the week connect,
the wind with the breath –
nothing that doesn't.

The broken heating plant in Żerań
and my child, and the woman
I picked out years ago because of
her white kneesocks with blue stripes.

Interesting, how the world
· connects tomorrow and the day after that.
If that's not it,
maybe you'll tell me what is.

[PS/DJE]

Days of the week

Tomorrow is Thursday.
If the world meets its obligations,
the following day will be Friday.
If it doesn't, it could even be Sunday,
and no one will ever guess
where our life got mislaid.

[PS/DJE]

Landscape with a branch

We are bound to one another
with unknown threads, a stitch
of red corpuscles sewing up the globe.
One day the globe
drops from us,
shrinks and dries
like a blackthorn plum –

something really was ours,
but we no longer belong to things.

[PS/EA]

Transparencies

The afternoon sun
round the corner of the town,
and every inch of skin
and every thought
is clearly exposed,
and nothing can be hidden
as everything comes to the surface:
unanswered letters,
ingratitude,
short memory.

[PS/DJE]

Innocence

When we first met, we were really so young.
I didn't see anything wrong in writing poems about myself.
Didn't I know that I too would be ashamed of something?
Didn't I know who you were?

Shame and laughter lock my mouth in turn.
I'm ashamed to think of it; I'm amused to be ashamed.

[PS/DJE]

Believe me

You're not going to find a better place
for these cosmetics, even if eventually
we wind up with some sort of bathroom cabinet and
you stop knocking them over with your towel –
there'll still be a thousand reasons to complain
and a thousand pieces of glass on the floor,
and a thousand new worries,
and we'll still have to get up early.

[PS/DJE]

Home and night

A day of sleeping and writing letters, of plasticine and games.
In place of dots the dominoes have animals,
crude shapes of animals on shoddy plastic.
A world without abstraction.
They cost sixty-eight złoties.
Everything's dearer and more primitive.
Could life by day really be less complicated?
Yes. But the dominoes are blue,
blue plastic with gold animals,
and life is black and white.

[PS/DJE]

Travel permit, round trip

A small calf on a cart, on cobblestones, happily whisking his tail, a Polish stork, lost in thought, a peasant woman wearing, as you'd expect, a kerchief on her head. A basket in her hand. The landscape rolls along at about the same pace, without stopping, and then illogically veils itself with hills.

I switch seats with a child who would rather watch the world unroll.

The tape is winding up somewhere on the other side and the reel must already be bulging. It contains so much, muck and beauty, the perpetual policemen, by trade and calling, stalking furiously, and these light-hearted village names: Pszczółki, Szymankowo.

My face may be still, but in my heart I'm bursting with laughter. One is again permitted to travel by train. The delicate pressure on my arm is only your sleep.

[1982]

[EV/PS]

Leaves and comes back

There's yet another life, being lived in brief, also unacknow-
ledged. A woman with a dog, a black poodle, outside the window
of Telimena on Krakowskie Przedmieście, passes by and vanishes,
as if she had no meaning. Life half imagined, half observed.

Vanishes, while from the opposite direction another elderly
woman appears, with a plastic bag; she must be going shopping.
But in the shop next door there's still no bread, and still no
papers at the kiosk. Yet everything's right today: the morning, the
imagination, the waitress bringing coffee, sight.

A little hedge in the square facing Dziekanka suddenly takes on
a different colour. Green, but more intense, and even the steel-
grey uniform of a militiaman – who, there's no knowing why, makes
towards the Mickiewicz monument – is more familiar, though not
quite mine. Perhaps he wants to take a closer look.

I don't know whether the world this autumn truly has more
dignity or whether it just seems so. Besides, memory is now
mingling: the gas in '68, the old dog Frendek licking up his own
blood, other months, other seasons.

I guess you can really put your life in order, can live with less.
But the heart, the heart doesn't give up easily, and goes on knock-
ing, and the eye, in its usual way, alters backgrounds and planes.
The tongue builds sentences, the body trembles slightly.

[1980-82]

[PS/DJE]

Medicine

Again I've seen a genuine lemon.
Ania brought it back for me from France.
She thought: return, or else stay on?
And what good reason holds her here –
a few faces, and words, and this anxiety?
The lemon was yellow and looked genuine.
No need to display it in the window
so it could come to itself, like our pale tomatoes,
or as we come to ourselves,
ripening and yellowing for years.
No, it was fully itself already
when she brought it, not so much yellow
as gold, and slightly gnarled.
So I accepted it gratefully.

I'd like to put on the thick skin of the world,
I'd like to be tart but on the whole tasty –
a child swallows me unwillingly,
and I help its cold.

[1981-82]

[PS/DJE]

A certain tree in Powązki cemetery

All memory we owe to objects
which adopt us for life and
tame us with touch, smell
and rustle. That's why it's so hard
for them to part with us: they guide us
till the end, through the world,
till the end they use us, surprised
by our coolness and the ingratitude
of that famous spinner Mnemosyne.

[PS/JA]

Fragility

I was going to sleep
not remembering a thing,
just scrunching up on the side of the bed,
knowing I should leave room.

I began the year washing dishes.
The water was warm, it was nobody's,
I didn't have to hurry.
Before my eyes

were all the verbs,
to be, to write, to love,
underfoot for years.
I didn't have to remember anything

although the mouth monotonously
repeated the word
memory, memory, memory
as if beyond it

nothing meant anything.
And, like it or not,
already on the edge of sleep,
I again saw your face

as it was a few hours back,
last year,
tired, but still beautiful,
dark blue like a swallow,

almost raven black,
and the face of a seven year old boy,
composed and delicate,
just about to smile;

your black hair
brightened against the child's light mop,
the mouth kept whispering memory, memory.
Drops of sleep ran down the pane of the eye.

[PS/JA]

Don't sleep, take notes

At four in the morning
the milkwoman was knocking,
in plain clothes, threatening
she wouldn't leave us anything,
at most remove the empties,
if I didn't produce the receipt.

It was somewhere in my jacket,
but in any case I knew
what the outcome would be:
she'd take away yesterday's curds,
she'd take the cheese and eggs,
she'd take our flat away,
she'd take away our child.

If I don't produce the receipt,
if I don't find the receipt,
the milkwoman will cut our throats.

[1981-82]

[PS/DJE]

Liberation, in language

These heart-stirring errors of craft;
uncertainty, how a nation
should respond to violence,
made up for by an urgent
sense of mission
(words big as beans
that are hard to swallow)
and that almost obsessive
lack of detail –

yes, one can speak this way
from the stage: this language
is not beautiful but all
abruptly draw out their hands
and clap, and so, perforce
it must be correct.

[PS/EA]

Worldliness

Hearing the lift coming up,
voices on the stairs, a brief argument,
the old dog is drawn away from her blanket
and the contemplation of another world,
and reluctantly strolls over to the door
to express her opinion. She favours
the worldly life, but without conviction.

[PS/DJE]

Talkativeness

But the citizen should be honest
and tell everything –
after all, the phones have been reconnected
so that he could
communicate with friends
or whoever he wants,
and it would be highly immoral
and, frankly speaking, quite unfair
to ring a friend
and not tell him everything
and in addition
to hint
that one knows much more

[1982]

[PS/DJE]

Grammar

What was, one should speak of in the past tense,
what isn't, in some other tongue.

[1982]

[PS/DJE]

Ah, continuity

This song might be right, pal,
but don't sing it to me again:
its refrain pulsing even in the roots
of pines, its echo hovering over the tips
of grass, its lyric fixed in the world's memory –
that dark horse of hope which says
nothing.

[1982]

[PS/MK]

Proofs

Don't worry about commas, all these
punctuation marks, colons, semi-colons
and dashes, which you so scrupulously
specify, will be, thanks to a proof-
reader's inattentiveness, left out; the rhythm
of your sentence, your thinking, your language
will prove less important than
you expected, or maybe than you wanted.
This was nothing but wishful thinking –
you won't be read to the music of speech
but to the hubbub of things.

[PS/DJE]

A small treatise on non-contradiction

Son goes out of the apartment block to get some air
since the Fall is still pretty, and why waste the weather.
He goes to the pond to study bugs, returns
and checks everything in books.

From the kitchen window I watch the boys kick a ball.
The door opens, and while the door's open
you can hear that today the elevator works,
clicks shut and moves on, to be useful.

[PS/MK]

A maple leaf

A maple leaf with the sun shining through it
at the end of summer is beautiful, but
not too much so, and even an ordinary
electric train passing by
nearly three hundred yards away
makes music, light and unobtrusive,
and yet to be remembered, for some sort of
usefulness perhaps, or even
instructiveness (the world somehow
doesn't quite say it knows everything,
has a good memory and, above all,
won't show it off).

[PS/JA]

FROM
A LATER WORLD
KOLEJNY ŚWIAT
(1983)

Space

(after Wang Wei)

We live secluded under the smoke of steelworks.
The area to the east and south is Warsaw.
The sun is burning out and shining through the dust.
The river is invisible, our house was built by little ants.
It's freezing and almost dark, white figures return to their homes.
The buses can hardly move –
at home dogs have had a hard day.

Today, just as before, there are unnecessary people.
But each of them can do a lot and bear a lot.

[PS/EA]

Another world

I talk about children all the time.
Tenderness and madness,
quiet answers to questions and their cries in dreams.
There are more of them and they're bigger and bigger,
they memorise whole books and reproduce them
turning pages, and drawing, drawing
even in the air, even with their fingers: trains,
three-cornered sails, trumpets, cymbals, the whole orchestra.
They say: you draw for me, you.

If one were born and lived somewhere else
one might not understand the fear of courage.

[PS/CM]

Hygiene

Today for the first time in months it stopped at one pack.
This is how it sounds best, when the impersonal form
gets into the ear by itself, when it speaks by itself.
Until recently the word "we" wasn't so annoying,
but just listen to something like this:
Today we have smoked only twenty.
Quite as if the author had asked for the floor
in order to announce the projected estimates of consumption in
       the current year,
whereas he wants to speak unasked.
So hang in there, boy, hang in there,
smoke, but not much; speak, but unobtrusively!

[PS/CM]

Potatoes

My son won't write a poem about a coconut.
I'm running out of words myself.
Still, if he wanted to paint a picture
with the texture of a ripe orange,
then by all means: let him get hold of a golden lemon,
and in a wink a warm wind
the colour of the setting sun will clothe it in a dress.
Imagination, mother of our life,
waft us more and more improbable landscapes!

[PS/CM]

In the provinces

The Municipal Cooperative For Housing Economy at Otwock
GREETS THE FRATERNAL NATIONS OF THE SOCIALIST COUNTRIES
with each of the forty-eight letters fixed on a separate pole,
only the spaces between the words have no posts.
It's May eleventh, 1979.
The poles stuck in the lawn form a breakwater.
The Municipal Cooperative has been greeting the brotherly nations
        for more than three weeks,
and to this day they don't know anything about it.

[PS/CM]

WHAT WE'RE REMEMBERED BY
PAMIĄTKI PO NAS
(1980)

First sentence

Four years ago at Ustka
four of us were walking on the sand, and
I began to write my second
story (the first had been
about an imagined
and painful death, very short
and a failure). I said the
first sentence to Maciek:
'Three years we waited, before
our applications for permission
to leave the beach were examined.'
He said it was a good start.
I don't remember what came later
or if there was any later, probably not.

I suppose I said that
simply because I thought it
effective, regardless of what
our favourite type of
humour was (a joke
could devour anything then).

I'm interested in knowing
if it was the truest fiction, and if
Maciek really believed
I was up to writing it, and
if it was indeed effective.

For why has he never
asked me: 'What about your story?'
And: 'Have you got a second sentence yet?' – That
might have encouraged me to work,
because I never liked to leave
people twisting in the wind.
And please consider, conditions
there were excellent – the place
had everything: beach, wind,
paper for the application, and thousands
of people, like me, hanging around
for someone to make up his mind.

This is certain

Young provincials have literary hopes.
They will follow their first lyrical impulses,
then they'll grow more bitter, but thanks to that, mature.
Lyric poetry, they believe, leads to an understanding
of themselves and the world, to perfection.
They'll look suspiciously upon the avant-garde,
and with some superiority, which will be reflected
in their modesty, their solid lyrical craft
and aspirations deliberately curtailed
(this much is certain: better a modest yet sound performance).

But they'll be full of enthusiasm.
And optimism.
Serious matters are at stake.
Far from the quarrels of the capital,
they know what to think.
There are always landscapes on their doorstep:
woods, a river, puffy pancakes of cloud,
or even wooden fences nibbled at by time.

There are places perhaps
where only what's good gets printed.
But that's an issue you can bypass and go to the field
through a hole in the fence, best of all on an autumn evening,
and look at the sky, or trees,
just about anything –
for everything reminds you of impermanence!

[PS/DD]

Old frame houses of Radość

'What's going on now?' –
It was a question
not addressed to me,
nor to my wife, nor
to the child, who had been asleep
for about two hours,
though asking it, Mother-in-law
turned her eyes on me.
It was a question to the world.

For a long time I said nothing,
but now the world
spoke through me.
It said: 'It's me –
Jacek Olszanka, the husband of your daughter –
who took the lid off the stove,
and put my old shoe
inside', whereupon
I left the kitchen
to grope my way
into the room with wife and child,
put the book aside
and once again rebuke you
with my profoundest
silence.

[PS/DJE]

A bit more effort, please
(to Krzysiek F.)

He could go to the Academy of Sciences now,
but says he's more relaxed –
in Świerk: an hour
of work, and then an hour
for himself; he can really
learn; besides, the computer is better.

During my month in London
I translated a few dozen poems
at the desk of the Gresham Hotel
in Bloomsbury Street, where
I was a receptionist,
so I know the work he has in mind.

We shall all further our education,
go from the desk
to the toilet, with a book
and a pencil, mark and memorise,
and come back so the boss
won't notice, until we become
one of the best-educated
nations in Central Europe.

[PS/DD]

Between bus stop and home
(to Pawel and Helena)

You go to visit your friend after a film screening,
your wife stayed at home alone,
your mother, you're beginning to think about
when you've stepped off the bus, is in another town,
ill, yesterday you had a telegram from her;
between the stop on the 140-A bus route
and your friend's home (passing, that is,
a closed shop; buying cigarettes
in the kiosk before the house; and even in the lift)
before you enter his flat and begin
the evening conversation with him and his wife, you're alone;
your child went to your wife's
parents yesterday, is alone,
without you and without his mother.
You think about all this before the door's opened,
as snow powders straight into your face, although
it is the third decade of March, pacing out
this short distance between bus stop and home.
Suddenly you notice this everyday loneliness, contrary to your self,
        perhaps,
and contrary to those you're thinking about.

[PS/DD]

Two gestures

A woman drags herself from bed.
You know, I think I ought to make myself some dinner.
But she doesn't have time
and dies between
two gestures: her mother's
and her child's, never discovering
who, or whose, she was
more.

[PS/DD]

Says the son

She thinks I'm leaving, but this is
as if blood were escaping
through clenched fingers. Blood
of blood. This is how she sees it though,
even if I'm always facing her
and we catch sight of ourselves in one another.
But the true mirror
is me, so pressed into the glass
that only a drop
trickling down is truer.
And I copy her light, and that
blood. I could reflect everything
in this way, except for a few words
for which she'll never forgive me.

[PS/DD]

Belated letter

Oh Grandpa César,
why didn't you wait for me?
A single glance would have been enough
and today I'd know that I can, that I have the right to
recall your face, because I'd really have seen it.
Photos are old and dead,
and Mother's stories rarer and rarer.
A single sentence would have been enough,
would have been repeated to me, for sure.

You know, Uncle Marcel – when I was there
for the first time – drew me the whole family tree
(I wanted to draw him one too,
but was ashamed: Mama, Grandma –
he already had Grandma anyway, since she was your wife –
Father, and Chaim and Fajga, his parents,
of whom, as about him, I know nothing to this day
– and that was everybody), and I looked and looked
surprised to find myself on this
big piece of paper, just below Mama,
and that in one family
there could be so many people.

You were of course much higher and deeper.
Everyone spoke of you
with respect and love, and I felt
that you had an artistic soul,
and I was proud.

I think that in a decent French family
in those days too, to marry
a Jew wasn't easy,
especially in a country
of which only the language was left
(although a friend says:
only the word *pan*, and the front porches).

Mama was saying there had been two
wedding ceremonies – I guess civil marriages
weren't so popular yet?–
ah, these compromises for the sake of the common good
and not irritating the relations, eh?
And when you came back from the war you supposedly
told Grandma to scramble twenty eggs.
That always impressed me an awful lot.

I wonder why you,
and not the other one, Father's father,
about whom I don't know a thing –
I don't know if it's possible to not know
so much about someone – except
that he lived, had a wife, a first and last name,
and that he had to do something.
So it would be even easier
to write about him, to him, than to you.
I could create myself, construct myself from scratch.
And what emotions those would be!

Was Łódź so grim a city back then too?
Of course. I'd bring you here, to Otwock,
and show you this place in detail,
where there's nothing to show, and would tell you.
Maybe this is where everything actually came from: there was nowhere
to go, nothing to see, one had to sit at home,
at most look out the window –
        fifty-, sixty-year-old frame houses, one or two floors of
        creaky stairs, exposed dumps and dead cats in the yards,
        and the ball that always gets away from the children into
        the garbage, some skinned pines, puddles, or dark dry stains
        after puddles, underwear on the line. All this – through
        the window and inside
        the tiled stove, the bed, the square of cellar-hatch on the floor,
        and the bronzed strip of sunlight lying under the wardrobe;
        dust.

My friends here don't know anything about you,
or maybe I did once mention
the *Legion d'honneur*, the mustachioed lieutenant, Verdun and the Somme,
but at most once, and probably only to one or two,

I forget whom.
And even if they remembered something of it,
they probably think I was boasting, who knows?
And maybe it really is making up one's own genealogy?

Later on, I was ashamed mostly
of not having learned your language.
Maybe Mama started to teach me too early,
when I preferred to grab a heel of bread
and go out to the yard (does it have to stay this way?
Colette once said I could speak
quite well). In the yard the children
reminded me too, calling
'piot-rhuzh, piot-rhuzh', as if they knew
and needed me to share their knowing
that you'd come from France. But soon
I realised it was a matter of another country,
that is, the other grandpa.
(I don't know how it happened that they
knew it so much better than I did then).
But I don't want to blame Mother, I myself
have wasted many an opportunity.

Oh Grandpa César,
why didn't you wait for me?
Your great-grandson hasn't turned three,
and yet if I died now, I bet
he'd remember something of me.
So just a few more years of life
would have been enough, a totally new world
for you to have to learn again,
these ten years, let's say: the end of the war,
Stalin, and at home
a son-in-law who, I think, hadn't finished the fourth form
in the *cheder*, a furrier, and finally me,
seven years after your death.
Mother preferred not to tell me
about Father's education, she was ashamed,
perhaps would have been even more ashamed in front of you.
Grandma didn't like him, supposedly,
I couldn't say, don't know
if it's people themselves who bear all the blame

for unhappy marriages.
(I remember once he made me a *kogel-mogel*,
but would only give it to me if I said I liked him more than Mother;
I don't know if she remembers,
I remember that shame.)

It's May, a few days ago
the first heavier rains fell.
And even every drop has its prehistory
which allows it to assume its own shape.
You know, at times it seems to me I am
a cluster of gestures which convinced me,
of words, which by some miracle I remembered
and quickly clutched
so they wouldn't get away, and of a few silences
I haven't learned.

Why am I doing this, indeed, why?
In fact there is no me for you even more
than no you for me,
though at least I know that you were
and that you died.
Why am I writing this letter, this poem, this I don't know what,
which wants to open me up from several sides
at once. Maybe it should
just find itself a natural ending
and not dawdle any longer, hang you in a frame
of memories, on the wall,
as your presumed portrait
(along with those twenty scrambled eggs, let's say,
or some other wheedled anecdote),
but it doesn't want to, it wants to go on with the theme
a little longer, as if you really were
only a literary pretext, broad enough
to let us talk about everything.

You know, today I was passing by
Grandma, that is, by you both
(forgive me, but I only just
realised that unless the graves
were confused, you're there together),
it was already dark, I'd taken a taxi

to get there before the child
whom I hadn't seen in a week, fell asleep.
I was riding by the wall
that divides the dead from the living
and I didn't know whether to believe
in life beyond the grave or not.
Is it indeed our children
who carry us further along? Some trace
should be left imprinted,
though one may well ask – what for.
And what does it mean to be faithful to oneself?

In a while I've got a conversation lesson
and should think up a subject to talk about,
since it's June already and the students
want to get into university.
Did you enjoy those private lessons, the girls
coming to your home – now
Więckowskiego Street, I guess, then what?
Did you have your real smile for them, and were the lessons
truly you?

What a coincidence that I do the same thing!
(Did you have to do it, too?)
Quite so, I smile
that it didn't come out all wrong, and keep collecting
all the pretexts for squeezing out words,
reasons for talking, for heavy moments of silence.
I remember writing a poem about this,
that didn't come off. Lately –
but I'm already in a bit of a rush – I write
only when it ought to come off,
or when I don't know what will, out of curiosity.
But am I myself really me?

And look, I've thought about it so much,
and it ends by itself.

[1976]

[PS/MK]

FROM THE AMERICAN
(1989)

Things to Translate

Walking

People here drive, and run, occasionally to death – sometimes unassumingly calling it jogging – and even go from one place to another, with a purpose in mind; walking is something forgotten or perhaps one day to be invented again.

Rich life, poor afterlife?

A small cemetery in the area (South Hadley?), with quite a few – in fact, many – Polish names; the earliest graves from the 1920s. If it had not been for the names, it would be hard to guess that all these people came from the Catholic part of Europe: where has all the richness and fantasy of the Catholic graveyards gone? Only the spaces which the graves take are bigger than in Europe, and the spaces between the graves, also bigger. The place looks austere and bare, spacious and empty, barely peopled.

Milking the wall

A phrase used in Polish by a Polish friend living in America, and translated, as it is, verbatim into English. Would probably have to be translated into English differently, to be understood in America? But at the same time, as it is, impossible to understand in Poland, since the automatic bank machines where one goes to withdraw some money when the bank is closed do not exist there.

Improper names

Transposing names and the way they sound – an improper thing to do perhaps? Even when they happen to belong to the category of so-called meaningful names? But the telephone directory, the Great Equaliser itself, the book revealing, if not quite visualising, a bit of the system we all know best, wants this done its own way. There are eight Marhefkas in it, all spelled with an "h" and an "f". All eight must be descendants of peasants who, at the turn of the century, came here from Poland, a place where they still spell the word with a "ch" and a "w", according to the rules of Polish spelling. 'Marchewka' means carrot. But this in English would have to be pronounced [ma:'tʃu:kə], in Polish a meaningless sound. In the family tradition, it has been clearly impossible to sacrifice sense and sound to spelling: all Marhefkas in the book, the way they sound and are pronounced in English, not the way they look on the page, still make sense, still mean carrots.

Forefathers, our representatives

A neighbour with a traceable Slavic name, this semester taking mainly maths courses, at UMass, half French (the mother), half Polish (the father), but born in America, where he is very likely to spend most of his life, going perhaps for holidays to France, where he will feel French, and where at his departure his French relatives will also treat him as their representative in America rather than an American. And he is likely to enjoy this doubleness, I suspect, even long after he stops being a maths student.

Meeting people

Some ultimate criterion of translatability: 'Had we met over there, would we be friends too?'

Among ourselves

A famous Polish writer I am being introduced to, in New York, just before a reading the three of us, Poles, are going to give there. He has been living in the States for nearly thirty years, but has not been read much, until recently, when he got that famous prize whose name people have generally heard. The other writer has been living in America for six years, and has not yet received any prize that people in this country could have heard of. There are three of us, Poles, in the room, but the host of the reading series is American, so our small talk happens in the lingua franca of today. The famous writer turns towards me and asks kindly in

English: 'Do you reside in Warsaw?' 'Yes,' I answer slowly, trying to gain time to understand what the problem could be – almost forty years away from Poland? certain old-fashionedness of diction? a difficulty in visualising those ugly cheap blocks of small flats most of us now live in, if we have been lucky enough to get them? my own inability to abstract from the somewhat different notion of "residing" or "residence" that for some reason sticks in my mind? – and then, still unable to decide, I quickly add: 'But I like the verb you used.' He laughs and – apparently feeling this is one of those misunderstandings that can be easily fixed – explains: 'You live in Warsaw, so it is the place of your residence.'

The zoo as text

One of the most amusingly innocent attitudes to translations – especially of poetry translations, perhaps – is trying to add explanatory words or phrases to what is being translated, an attempt to incorporate footnotes into the integrity of the text of the original. This is frequently accompanied by the implied notion that nothing has really been violated. After all, is this not being done with good intentions? for the benefit of the reader? so that the reader could understand better? As, clearly, otherwise the reader would not have the slightest idea what to think. Therefore every spot of the text demanding on the part of the reader a little bit of effort, some more active reading, a bit of homework, is going to be levelled, or footnoted within. Why should you wear yourself out giving birth, honey, if you can get a caesarian?

Examples of such overtranslations can be found anywhere. I found one in a particular enumeration, before the cage of Moustached Guenon, in the San Diego Zoo. It went, with the first three words capitalised, as follows: 'Please do not: annoy, torment, pester, plague, molest, worry, badger, harry, harass, heckle, persecute, irk, bullyrag, vex, disquiet, grate, beset, bother, tease, nettle, tantalise, or ruffle the animals.' Suddenly, all my ability to judge and distinguish between the so-called good and bad, the whole instinct of taste almost – was questioned. And I felt as if I were being grossly mistranslated to the animals.

A song

What shall we do with all our untranslated diacritical marks?

Untranslatability of squirrels

The grey ones in Amherst seem faded sometimes, as if indeed they once lost their more or less fiery-red colour, the intensity of which may depend on the sun and season, the colour so characteristic for the squirrels in Eastern Europe. In the old Łazienki Park in Warsaw there are plenty of them, and people try to feed them from their hands, unlike the way they feed the monstrously huge carp in the Park's royal pond, where people simply throw the food in. Supposedly, the most effective way to make the squirrel come close, is to call out gently, several times, one time after another: 'Basia-Basia-Basia', a more intimate version of the name Barbara. The name – or maybe the quality of its sound – is for some reason supposed to be more familiar to the squirrel than some less rustling Polish names. But the grey, kindly disposed Amherst squirrel of Amity Street, turns round and leaves us alone with our good intentions, unimpressed by our rhubarb literals: 'Barbara-Barbara-Barbara'.

Piotr Sommer was born in 1948 in Wałbrzych, Poland. He graduated from the University of Warsaw in 1973. Since 1976 he has worked for the Warsaw magazine *Literatura na świecie* (World Literature). He is also associated with two other magazines: *Res Publica* and *Tygodnik Literacki* (Literary Weekly). In 1987-89 he taught, as a visiting writer and visiting professor, at several American colleges and universities, including Amherst College, Mount Holyoke College, Wesleyan University and the University of Nebraska-Lincoln. In 1991 he was visiting translator at Warwick University in England.

He has published several books of poems in Polish: *W krześle* (1977), *Pamiątki po nas* (1980), *Kolejny świat* (1983), *Czynnik liryczny* (1986) and *Czynnik liryczny i inne wiersze* (1988). He also writes poems for children (*Przed snem*, 1981), translates contemporary American, English and Irish poetry into Polish, and writes literary criticism. Among other translations, he has published *Antologia nowej poezji brytyjskiej* (an anthology of new British poetry, 1983), a book of his interviews with British poets, *Zapisy rozmów* (1985), and a selection of poems by Frank O'Hara (1987). He is currently working on a Polish selection of poems by Charles Reznikoff. *Things to Translate* (Bloodaxe Books, 1991), is his first book to be published in English.

AUTHORS PUBLISHED BY

BLOODAXE BOOKS

FLEUR ADCOCK
ANNA AKHMATOVA
SIMON ARMITAGE
NEIL ASTLEY
SHIRLEY BAKER
GEREMIE BARMÉ
MARTIN BELL
CONNIE BENSLEY
YVES BONNEFOY
GORDON BROWN
BASIL BUNTING
CIARAN CARSON
ANGELA CARTER
JOHN CASSIDY
JAROSLAV ČEJKA
MICHAL ČERNÍK
SID CHAPLIN
RENÉ CHAR
GEORGE CHARLTON
EILÉAN NÍ CHUILLEANÁIN
KILLARNEY CLARY
JACK CLEMO
JACK COMMON
STEWART CONN
NOEL CONNOR
DAVID CONSTANTINE
JENI COUZYN
HART CRANE
ADAM CZERNIAWSKI
PETER DIDSBURY
MAURA DOOLEY
JOHN DREW
IAN DUHIG
HELEN DUNMORE
DOUGLAS DUNN
STEPHEN DUNSTAN
G.F. DUTTON
LAURIS EDMOND
STEVE ELLIS
ODYSSEUS ELYTIS
CHARLOTTE EVEREST-PHILLIPS
RUTH FAINLIGHT
RICHARD FALKNER

EVA FIGES
SYLVA FISCHEROVÁ
TONY FLYNN
VICTORIA FORDE
TUA FORSSTRÖM
JIMMY FORSYTH
LINDA FRANCE
ELIZABETH GARRETT
ARTHUR GIBSON
PAMELA GILLILAN
ANDREW GREIG
JOHN GREENING
PHILIP GROSS
JOSEF HANZLÍK
TONY HARRISON
DOROTHY HEWETT
FRIEDRICH HÖLDERLIN
MIROSLAV HOLUB
FRANCES HOROVITZ
DOUGLAS HOUSTON
PAUL HYLAND
KATHLEEN JAMIE
VLADIMÍR JANOVIC
B.S. JOHNSON
JOOLZ
JENNY JOSEPH
SYLVIA KANTARIS
JACKIE KAY
BRENDAN KENNELLY
SIRKKA-LIISA KONTTINEN
JEAN HANFF KORELITZ
DENISE LEVERTOV
HERBERT LOMAS
MARION LOMAX
EDNA LONGLEY
FEDERICO GARCÍA LORCA
PETER McDONALD
DAVID McDUFF
OSIP MANDELSTAM
GERALD MANGAN
E.A. MARKHAM
JILL MAUGHAN
GLYN MAXWELL

HENRI MICHAUX
JOHN MINFORD
JOHN MONTAGUE
EUGENIO MONTALE
DAVID MORLEY
VINCENT MORRISON
RICHARD MURPHY
SEAN O'BRIEN
JULIE O'CALLAGHAN
JOHN OLDHAM
TOM PAULIN
GYÖRGY PETRI
TOM PICKARD
DEBORAH RANDALL
IRINA RATUSHINSKAYA
DIANE RAWSON
MARIA RAZUMOVSKY
JEREMY REED
CAROL RUMENS
EVA SALZMAN
WILLIAM SCAMMELL
DAVID SCOTT
JO SHAPCOTT
JAMES SIMMONS
MATT SIMPSON
DAVE SMITH
KEN SMITH
EDITH SÖDERGRAN
PIOTR SOMMER
MARIN SORESCU
LEOPOLD STAFF
PAULINE STAINER
MARTIN STOKES
KAREL SÝS
RABINDRANATH TAGORE
JEAN TARDIEU
R.S. THOMAS
TOMAS TRANSTRÖMER
MARINA TSVETAYEVA
ALAN WEARNE
NIGEL WELLS
C.K. WILLIAMS
JOHN HARTLEY WILLIAMS

*For a complete list of poetry, fiction, drama and photography books
published by Bloodaxe, please write to:*

**Bloodaxe Books Ltd, P.O. Box 1SN,
Newcastle upon Tyne NE99 1SN.**